Special
Gift

for:

Lacey Collins

from:

Liana & Kate Baker

date:

May 2004

Dedication

To my three sons,
Taylor,
Riley, &
Spencer
—who will be graduates
all too soon!

So, don't be anxious about tomorrow.

Stories, sayings, and scriptures to Encourage and Inspire the . . . .

hugs™

for Grads

HOWARD
PUBLISHING CO.

EFF WALLING

rsonalized Scriptures by
EANN WEISS

So, don't be an
about tomor

Holiness Hope

Our purpose at Howard Publishing is to:

- *Increase faith* in the hearts of growing Christians
- *Inspire holiness* in the lives of believers
- *Instill hope* in the hearts of struggling people everywhere

Because He's coming again!

Hugs for Grads © 2001 by Jeff Walling
All rights reserved. Printed in the United States of America

Published by Howard Publishing Co., Inc.,
3117 North 7th Street, West Monroe, LA 71291-2227

03 04 05 06 07 08 09 10   10 9 8 7 6

Personalized scriptures by LeAnn Weiss, owner of Encouragement Company,
3006 Brandywine Dr., Orlando, FL 32806; 407-898-4410

Edited by Philis Boultinghouse
Interior design by Stephanie Denney

Library of Congress Cataloging-in-Publication Data
Walling, Jeff, 1957-
   Hugs for grads : stories, sayings, and scriptures to encourage and inspire the— / Jeff
Walling ; personalized scriptures by LeAnn Weiss.
      p. cm.
   ISBN 1-58229-155-1
   1. High school graduates—Conduct of life. 2. Young adults—Conduct of life. 3.
High school graduates—Religious life. 4. Young adults—Religious life. 5. Christian
life. I. Weiss, LeAnn. II. Title.

BJ1661 .W28 2001
248.8'3—dc21

                                                                    00-048223

Contents

Chapter 1

Holding On

Live your life Worthy
of the calling
you have received from Me.
I know the plans I have for you.

Trust Me.

I have plans to prosper you
and not to harm you,
plans to give you hope
and a future!

When you seek Me with all
your heart, you'll find Me.
You can count on Me
to faithfully complete the
good work I started in you.

Love,
Your God of Purpose

—from Ephesians 4:1; Jeremiah 29:11–14; Philippians 1:6

Traditions can be either the links that connect one generation to the next or the shackles that hold us back from the future. Without a connection to our past, we lose part of who we are and how God has shaped us through the blessings and trials we've faced. But if we cling slavishly to "how it has always been," we will lose the dreams and ideas that are the hope for tomorrow.

What part will traditions play in your life? That is one of the greatest choices you will make as you embark on this next phase of living. Learning to embrace tradition as the connection to your roots while using it as the steppingstone to your dreams is the challenge of a lifetime. As you do, you will build your own traditions to pave the road to your tomorrow.

Thank you, Lord, for the bless-ings of my past and the tradi-tions that have shaped my life. Guide me as I build my own traditions and celebrate the possibilities of my future.

The past does not have to be your prison. You have a voice in your destiny. You have a say in your life. You have a choice in the path you take. Choose well and someday—generations from now—your grandchildren and great-grandchildren will thank God for the seeds you sowed.

—Max Lucado

graduation

Three weeks before
graduation day,
she made her
last stand.

Three weeks before
graduation day,
she made her
last stand.

Staying Connected

"Dad, I need to tell you something."

Jean had rehearsed the speech for hours and was determined to get through it without breaking down. She bit her lip and prepared to plow ahead when the wind blew the tassel from her mortarboard right in her face, distracting and frustrating her. *Who thought up these stupid tassels anyway?* Jean pondered as she adjusted the cap for the thousandth time. She wasn't much for formality: All the pomp and circumstance was so overblown. But Dad was big on tradition and ritual.

"Don't you see, Jeanie," he had often lectured her; "tradition is what holds families together. Without it you have no connection between the generations, nothing to help hold you to what came before."

And her dad definitely wanted her connected: Every family reunion at the farm in Tennessee meant a mandatory appearance by the West Coast wing of the McGee clan. Jean's dad and mom had both grown up in that small Tennessee town, and all her uncles and aunts still lived within a hour's drive of the family farm. Though her dad still called it "home," he hadn't lived there since graduating from high school. A scholarship to a big California college was too good to refuse, so he'd married Jean's mom two days after graduation and then moved to the Sunshine State, where Jean and her little brother had been born. The rest of the McGees predicted that Jean's family would lose their ties to Tennessee, but every summer that Jean could remember had included a trip to the farm and visiting all the relatives. Dad wanted them to know every cousin, aunt, and uncle by name. "This is your heritage," Dad would say when anyone complained about trips. "You have to stay connected!"

"Do you miss the farm, Dad?" Jeanie had once asked her father as they were starting the long drive back to California.

"Wouldn't you?" That was Dad—answer a question with a question. "I learned to drive a tractor, bale hay, and ride a horse on that farm. Why I remember when..." If Jeanie would just sit tight, Dad would roll through one of his stories: The time Uncle Willie had nailed his brother's hat to the farmhouse floor to teach him not to be sloppy. Or the day Aunt Mildred nearly blew up the place when the pressure cooker got too hot while she was canning peaches.

Although Jean had loved listening to those stories as a child, she had no interest in them now. It was one more sign of the gulf that had come between her and her dad: Mr. Tradition versus Miss New Age. From burning incense in her room to a tattoo on her ankle, every issue became an argument. The year she ditched the family reunion for her boyfriend's rock band's concert had nearly seen her booted from the house. Only her mom's intercession had spared her from excommunication.

But then came the graduation thing.

Jean had been adamant: She was not taking part in the ceremonies. Her friends had applauded her independent thinking. "The cap-and-gown thing is an unnecessary, outdated custom," they had agreed. But needless to say, her dad saw it differently and was ready to push the issue. Three weeks before graduation day, she made her last stand. The announcements were lying on the hall table waiting to be addressed, and her cap and gown were already hanging in the closet. She dropped the bomb at dinnertime: "I've decided I am not wearing that silly cap and gown and going through that lame ceremony," she had casually said between bites; then she had added defiantly, "And there's nothing you can do about it."

Her dad's ears had gone crimson, and her mother just held her breath. After a moment of painful silence, Jean's mother picked up her dinner, nodded to Sammy, Jean's little brother, and quietly left the dining room. Sammy took his cue and gathered up his plate as well, saying, "I guess nobody will gripe if I eat in my room tonight." And with that the two combatants were left alone to duke it out.

Jeanie's dad began with a predictable response: "What do you think this says to your family?" When she did not respond, he continued, "Your grandmother and all the folks from back home will be here to see you graduate. It means a lot to them…and to me. Please, don't be so selfish!"

"Well, it means something to me too. I'm sorry, Dad, but I'm not backing down."

"I suppose you won't want the watch either," he had said softly.

She knew this was coming, but it made her mad that he brought it up so quickly.

"Oh, Dad, don't start with that."

"The watch" was a gold pocket watch. When her paternal grandfather had graduated from high school, the first McGee to do so, his father hadn't been able to afford a proper graduation gift, so he gave him a family heirloom, that pocket watch. That watch had been passed down from generation to generation for six decades and was always given to the eldest child at his or her graduation. Jean was the eldest McGee of her generation.

"So if I don't wear the cap and gown, I don't get the watch? Is that it?"

Her dad just shook his head, and that had been the end of the graduation conversation…until now.

The wind was getting chillier, and the ceremony was only a half-hour away. She knew if she didn't get this said now, she might never, so she started again. "Dad, this may seem strange, but I need to say this." She paused and soaked up the silence. Her father would not interrupt her.

She adjusted the cap one last time and couldn't help but grin. Here she stood in the goofy cap and gown she'd sworn she'd never wear, all ready to get her diploma in front of her relatives. But not because her father had bullied her into it. Far from it. Three days after the dinner argument, her dad had come to her room at bedtime and offered an olive branch.

"Listen, I'm tired of being mad about this. I know you're

a bright girl and that you'll make your own way. Maybe it's time I let you do so." And with that, he had laid the pocket watch on her bed and walked out.

The wind blew the tassel across her eyes one more time, but she barely noticed. The tears she had fought back so fiercely now flowed freely…and she didn't care. Somehow, she kept talking.

"Dad, I want you to know why I'm doing this. It's not just because of what happened. I've thought a lot about tradition in the last two weeks. About staying connected. You never told me that it would become so much more important when…things were different."

She wiped the tears back and held out the watch.

"I'm going to carry this when I get my diploma. And one day I'm gonna give it to my child, if I'm lucky enough to have one. And I want to tell my children to stay connected to their history, their family. I want to tell them about you…I love you, Daddy. And I'm sorry."

There! She had said it. Those words had burned in her brain for the last ten days, ever since the phone call about her dad's accident and the painful meeting with her mother at the hospital. She knew she needed to say them, but her dad hadn't been able to hear them. The doctors weren't even sure if he was really alive when the ambulance brought him in: The drunk driver had hit him head-on.

"Good-bye, Daddy," she said softly as she laid a small piece of paper on her father's headstone. Then Jean turned from the grave, walked back to the car, and drove to meet the rest of family at her graduation. A gust of wind gently spun the paper on the smooth granite, as though an unseen hand was turning it around to read it: It was her graduation announcement.

Chapter 2

Trusting Truth

Godliness has Value for
all areas of your life,
holding promise
for both now and eternity.
Follow My formula
for Success by growing in
diligence, faith, moral excellence,
knowledge, self-control,
perseverance, godliness,
brotherly kindness, and love.
For as long as these qualities are yours
and are increasing, you'll always
be fruitful and productive
in the equation of life.

LOVE,
YOUR CREATOR

—from 1 Timothy 4:8; 2 Peter 1:4–11

There are voices in the world that suggest that right and wrong are passé, that notions like good and evil are fit only for children's stories. This is not so.

God has placed an economy in this universe that successful people use to guide their choices. It recognizes that right and wrong, good and evil are not arbitrary forces that change with the times. They are as constant as $2 + 2 = 4$. Learning the immutable laws of life is the greatest education one can attain. Though the truth is not always as clear as a mathematical equation, knowing what is right and seeking to do it will never lead to a faulty answer.

Look for the constants as you walk the path of life. Memorize them as you would a chart of formulas, and they will come in handy again and again as you face the complex decisions that will make up your tomorrow.

Teach me, oh Lord, to number my days that I may gain a heart of wisdom.

The simple basics of life—love, faith, and hope—are all we really need. We can't undo all the world's wrongs, but we can affect the corner of the world we live in if we'll just stick to the basics— the basics of life.

—Kirk Sullivan, 4HIM

results

"If you keep doing the same thing, the same way, you will keep getting the same results."

"If you keep doing the same thing, the same way, you will keep getting the same results."

By the Numbers

"Anybody home?" Shannon called as she stuck her head into room 216.

The room smelled of chalk dust and dry paper, and Shannon couldn't shake the old feeling that she should have studied harder for the test she was about to take. But there was no test today. The school year at Redlands High had officially ended almost twenty-four hours ago. And besides that, it had been two years since she had been a student in Mr. Schiller's algebra class.

Her family had moved to Redlands from Cleveland the summer before her sophomore year. Her father's transfer had been sudden, and Shannon had barely had time to say her good-byes before the moving van arrived. But if the truth were known, there weren't that many good-byes to be said. Her family's constant moves kept her friendships few and shallow. And her older brother's athletic talents kept Shannon securely in the shadows. Buck was the star quarterback, first-string center, and ace relief pitcher—the kind of kid that high-school legends are made of. Shannon was always "Buck's sister." But she didn't begrudge her brother the fame; she did what most kids do in that spot: accept it quietly and look for some place she could excel.

And that's where Mr. Schiller, her algebra teacher, came into her life. Schiller was a first-generation German immigrant. Nearly seventy years old, he always dressed in a starched-white, long-sleeved shirt and a tie—the picture of efficiency and predictability. It was rumored that his father had been in the German army, but Mr. Schiller always deflected questions about his father with the same response: "That was a long time ago. Today is what matters."

But there was one subject you couldn't keep him quiet

about: math. He was passionate about numbers, and that passion attracted Shannon in a strange way. When Mr. Schiller talked about formulas or equations, you would think he were describing a long-lost love. Some students dubbed him the "Math Nazi," but Shannon found the elderly man to be a model teacher. His class was like another world. When you came into his classroom, it didn't matter who you were or where you were from. In room 216, the only thing that mattered was the numbers...and getting them right.

Shannon had her share of trouble getting the numbers right. She had nearly flunked two of Mr. Schiller's quizzes and was on her way to her first F in her high-school career when he asked her to stay after class one Friday.

"You don't like algebra, do you, Miss Hauptmann?" Mr. Schiller asked.

"I wouldn't say that. I just can't seem to get it."

"Oh you can get it, Miss Hauptmann. You just have to do it by the numbers."

"I'm trying to, Mr. Schiller."

"Really. Let's just see how you are trying." He picked up the chalk and began to write on the board: $F = C + H$

"Would you please solve this equation?" Shannon looked confused. Mr. Schiller let her stew a moment and then picked up the chalk again. "How many hours of class time have we had in algebra this semester?"

"Uh," Shannon stuttered, "I have no idea."

"Yes you do. Think about the numbers! Forty-five minutes each day, five days a week, for six weeks. How much is that?" Before Shannon could protest, he had the chalk in her hand and was guiding her through the simple calculations. $C = (45 \times 5 \times 6) / 60$. She wrote the answer on the board, *22.5 hours,* and tried to hand the chalk back.

"Oh no, we are not finished yet. Now, how many hours do you give to math homework each night?" Shannon thought quietly. Mr. Schiller sat on the edge of his desk watching her, then he added, "The truth, Miss Hauptmann, will set you free."

"I guess I spend about fifteen minutes a night...on average."

"All right then, how many hours have you spent in total on math homework so far this semester?" The answer was obvious: In the first six weeks of the semester, Shannon had invested only seven and a half hours in homework.

"So the equation looks like this." Mr. Schiller wrote in broad, clear strokes on the board.

F = 22.5 hours + 7.5 hours

"The numbers do not lie, Miss Hauptmann. If you keep doing the same thing, the same way, you will keep getting the same results. The question is, What part of that equation do you want to change?"

"Well, I'm sure not excited about bringing home an F," Shannon responded.

"Then you must get excited about the numbers! If you want to change this F to an A, then start by changing this." Mr. Schiller circled the number of hours she had studied. "Why don't we try a little experiment, you and I. You change this 7.5 to, say, 15 hours over the next six weeks. You understand what that means?"

"I would have to double the time I spend on math every night."

"That's right! You do it by the numbers, and I will throw out those first two quiz grades, and we'll see what results you get? Deal?"

"Deal." As they shook hands, Shannon couldn't help smiling: This man was into his math. And soon, so was Shannon. She found herself more than doubling her study time and even reading ahead to the concepts that were coming up next. And Mr. Schiller stoked the fires of her interest with little cryptic notes of encouragement on her homework: "The numbers don't lie!" or "Trust the numbers!"

By the end of the first semester, Shannon had a solid A in algebra.

Over the rest of that school year, Shannon made more visits to room 216 after school, but none of them was mandatory. She would drop by just to chat—first, about math, and then, about life. Shannon found it amazingly easy

to talk with him about her problems. He would speak per-
suasively of the importance of making good choices and the
responsibilities of freedom. And he would always turn her
problems into equations. The time she had gotten in trouble
at home for lying to her mother he had drawn this equation:

$TRUST = H + T$

"You have lost a terrible thing," he had said, staring over
the glasses that always rode nearly at the edge of his pointed
nose. "You've lost the *trust* your mother had in you. When
you lied to her, you destroyed the trust you had built up in
your relationship."

"But how do I get that back?" Shannon asked.

"By the numbers, Shannon: *Trust* is equal to *honesty* over
time. You must be consistent and honest with your parents
over time for that trust to be regained. There is no short-cut
—the equation is unchangeable."

And Mr. Schiller had been right. He had an equation for
just about everything, and they all made sense. As she grew
in her respect for Mr. Schiller, she grew in her confidence in
herself. While Buck received a sizable football scholarship at

UCLA, Shannon had enjoyed deciding which of the four universities that were vying for her attention she would attend. Mr. Schiller even helped her to develop a chart to rate each one over a number of areas. As usual, his formula proved valuable. She would begin at Massachusetts Institute of Technology in the fall with all her tuition covered by math scholarships. She had dropped by on the last day of school to share the good news with her math mentor, but he had already left the campus. So she had gone by the next day on the chance that she might find him cleaning out his room.

"Hello, Mr. Schiller? Anybody home?"

A pair of glasses perched on a pointed nose appeared from behind the desk. "Shannon! I'm so glad you came by. Did MIT come up with the numbers?"

"Oh boy, did they—nearly 20 percent more than I had expected. Thanks for all your help, Mr. Schiller."

"Helping others is what makes life add up!"

Mr. Schiller stood up, and Shannon noticed that he had rolled up the sleeves of the old blue work shirt he was wearing. She had never before seen him so casually dressed and was about to comment on it when she noticed something on his left arm. It was a set of numbers tattooed in his flesh.

Mr. Schiller caught her gaze and quickly covered the numbers with his other hand. He turned to pick up another box of papers and carried them to a closet in the corner. Shannon stood quietly, thinking through what she had just seen. Schiller hadn't been a Nazi—he had been in a Nazi concentration camp. He was a German Jew. Now all those lectures on freedom and responsibility made so much more sense. The silence grew awkward, and it was Mr. Schiller who finally broke it.

"For a long time I hated numbers. I swore I would run from them, rid my life of them. Strange, no? I have given my life to them instead."

"No, sir. You have not given your life to numbers." Shannon said gently. "Numbers don't mean anything. It's the people who use them that make all the difference. Mr. Schiller, I don't know what you went through to get those numbers on your arm, but you had every right to be bitter and cynical about this world."

"That is true," Mr. Schiller agreed.

"But you weren't. You chose to care for me and hundreds of other students who learned from you. You taught us more than numbers. You taught us to do it right. To be right. You know what I'm going to be majoring in at MIT?"

Mr. Schiller just shook his head.

"Math. I want to be a math teacher who changes the world by the numbers: one student at a time."

Mr. Schiller smiled as a solitary tear rolled down his cheek. "And so you will, Miss Hauptmann. And so you will."

Chapter

3

Growing
through
Giving

When you feel OVERwhelmed
and at the end of yourself,
look up and remember that

your help comes from ME!
See My power perfected
in your weakness.
I am able to
abundantly stockpile you with
all grace and sufficiency
so that you will have more than enough
for every good deed I call you to.
When you love Me
and are called according to
My purpose,
I cause all things to work together
for your benefit.

MY ALL-SUFFICIENT GRACE,
YOUR FAITHFUL GOD

—from Psalm 121:1–2; 2 Corinthians 12:9; 9:8; Romans 8:28

Weakness is no one's goal. Strength and might are the twin companions of victory. Yet grief and loss are the ambassadors of growth and the harbingers of wisdom. They reveal what would otherwise have been hidden and bring into sharp relief the reality that is life. They provide the contrast that makes the bright days brighter, and they bring the humility that allows us to handle later victories well.

So do not despise

the broken wing, the shattered dream, or the dashed hope. For though they bring tears and grief, they prepare you for a dream unseen, a hope unimagined. Look behind the tragedy, and you are likely to find an opportunity to bless and be blessed. Anything less, and the pain will have been wasted. That is the definition of true tragedy.

Dear God, show me the lessons in my weakness and the path to service through my pain.

Love cures people, the
ones who receive love and
the ones who give it, too.
—Karl A. Menninger

Sheila had figured
that if she could get
thirty pills
and take them
all at once,
that would do it.

Something about Mary

Sheila smiled as she pulled into the handicap parking space behind the school gym. Parking was one of the few things that had actually gotten easier since being confined to a wheelchair. She unlatched her chair from the brace that held it in front of the steering wheel of her van and rolled back onto the lift that lowered her to the sidewalk. She smiled again, thinking how second nature all this had become in just three months.

It had been a muggy morning in August when she had stepped off the curb at Harris Avenue and into the path of a Toyota truck. As usual, she had been well ahead of the rest of the girls cross-country team as they went through the daily rigors of the summer training. Only Kim Miller had been close enough to actually see the accident. "It looked like you were an angel…flying," she had told Sheila later in the hospital.

And indeed she had flown—thirty-six feet, according to the police report. The doctors called it a miracle that she had survived, and Sheila's church prayed nonstop for the first forty-eight hours that she was in the coma. Once she came to, they prayed that she would be able to run again. That prayer was not to be answered. Three of the vertebrae in Sheila's lower back had been smashed to powder. The pressure had nearly severed the spinal cord, and she had no feeling or control of the lower half of her body.

For three months she had awoken each morning praying it was all a bad dream. But soon her prayer changed: "If I can't walk again, God, let me die." But even that request went unanswered: Her heart was in good condition, and the doctors patiently assured her that she could live a "normal life"…in a wheelchair. Sheila decided she would answer her own prayer. She quietly began saving up the pain pills that the evening nurse at the rehabilitation center grudgingly gave her when she complained that she could not sleep. Sheila had figured that if she could get thirty of them and take them all at once, that would do it. Thirty days. That's all it would take.

It was on the twenty-eighth day that Mary Johnson spilled urine all over Sheila's lap.

"What are you doing!" Sheila shouted as the warm yellow liquid squirted from her "leg bag" and onto her white shorts.

"Ooooh, I am so sorry, miss. I've messed up again." Mary was trying to stop the flow of the urine, but her attempts to pull the bag away just made it squirt more.

"You idiot. Let it go, just let it go!" Sheila swatted Mary's hands away from the bag and then pinched the end of the tube tightly. "You have to undo that strap and clamp it before you can take it off. Don't you know that?"

"I'm so sorry, ma'am, I should have waited for Mrs. Bannister to help me. Please don't say nothing," Mary's eyes pleaded. "I just started yesterday, but I ain't gonna make it. I know that."

"Hey, a little pee on the floor isn't the worst thing that can happen to a girl."

Mary wiped at her eyes and then stooped to wipe the side of Sheila's chair and the puddle of urine on the floor beside it. "Stupid is as stupid does," she said softly.

Sheila looked at the young black woman with interest. "What's your name?"

"You want to know so you can report me?"

"Relax, I just want to know so I won't be saying 'Hey, girl-that-made-me-pee-myself, how's it going?' "

Mary looked at Sheila skeptically and then grinned a charming, bright smile. "Mary. Mary Johnson's my name. But my friends call me Queenie." She stuck out her hand, and Sheila shook it.

"I'm Sheila Taylor. But my friends call me Cripple." Mary looked shocked. "Ah, just kidding. Actually, my friends don't call nearly as much as they used to. They're all getting on with their lives, I guess."

"I'm sorry." Mary said, and her eyes strayed to the cards from the track team and the pictures from some of her races that were tacked on the wall above her bed.

"Did you go to Central High?" Sheila asked.

"No," Mary said quickly and went about emptying the remainder of the leg bag into the commode in Sheila's rest room.

"So where did you go to high school?"

"Nowhere. My dad got killed when some gang-bangers robbed the corner store while he was in it," Mary said matter-of-factly as she returned the leg bag to Sheila's chair. "My mom was sick, so I went to work. I left seventh grade and never went back."

Sheila pondered this a moment and could think of nothing to say in response. When Mary had finished her work, she turned to face Sheila. "I'm sorry again for the mess. If they don't fire me today, I'll try to do better tomorrow." And with that she left.

That night Sheila counted her pills again: twenty-nine. She tucked them under her mattress and closed her eyes. One more and she could kiss all of this good-bye.

"Good morning, Sheila!" Sunlight poured through the windows as Mary pulled back the drapes.

"I see they didn't fire you," Sheila moaned as she swung her lifeless legs off the bed.

"Not yet. The head nurse told me you're supposed to be going back to school in another six weeks."

"Yeah, right. What a thrill."

Mary stared again at the pictures of Sheila with her high-school friends. "I always thought that someday I'd go back. I used to imagine what it would feel like to walk up in front of everybody to get a diploma."

"So what's keeping you from doing it?" Sheila asked as Mary helped her into her wheelchair.

"I tried once. Never could pass the English test." She stooped to carefully loosen Sheila's leg bag and then emptied it in the rest room. "Can't read worth a lick. I couldn't take time to go back to school, and I just haven't got the brains to do it on my own."

Sheila rolled to the window and, stretching her arms, yawned loudly. "Sounds like you need to get yourself a tutor."

"Can't afford one. And who's got the time to do it for free."

Something in her voice touched Sheila deep within. After no more than a moment's thought, she said: "Say, Queenie. How would you like to graduate?"

With just five months till graduation, it wouldn't be easy, but something about Mary gave Sheila energy. Her pile of pills under the mattress was soon forgotten, and beginning that day, Sheila focused all her will power on helping Mary Johnson graduate from high school. She contacted her guidance counselor, got a copy of the English textbook, and began to tutor Mary.

When the supervisors at the rehab center learned of Sheila's project, they gave Mary extra time each day to work with her "tutor." The study sessions weren't always easy. "I'm too old for this," Mary said after getting back an essay covered with corrections from Sheila's red pen. "I'm nearly thirty-four!"

"And I'm in a wheelchair! Get over it and rewrite that essay," Sheila shot back with a grin. They worked hard for six weeks, but when it came time for Sheila to leave the rehab, Mary was still not ready for the exam: She failed three practice tests and seemed ready to throw in the towel.

"Let's admit it," Mary said, "this is one race you just ain't going to win."

"Don't you count us out yet, girl," Sheila said. When she got her specially equipped van, Sheila had to start back to school as well. But three days a week after class, she would swing by the center and work with Mary.

With only two weeks to go till graduation, it was time for Mary to sit for the real test. "Just don't get pee on anybody, and you'll do great!" she had whispered to Mary as she entered the examination hall. That had been seventy-two agonizing hours ago. Mary was to get the results of the test that very afternoon, and they had agreed that if she passed, she would meet Sheila here, behind the gym, and walk behind her to receive her diploma.

Sheila peered at the crowd of seniors in caps and gowns gathering at the gym's rear door. Mary was nowhere to be seen. The band was beginning to play, and the other seniors were lining up. As Sheila rolled toward her place in line, she fought back tears. She knew that Mary might not pass. The exam was a tough one. She even thought about leaving the ceremony altogether, but her family was there to watch her roll across the platform, and she didn't want to disappoint them.

As the marching music began, Sheila started to roll her chair, but it wouldn't budge. She checked the brakes and then pushed again, but the chair stayed stuck. Then a hand tapped her on the shoulder. "You weren't thinking of going without me, were you?" Mary stood behind her, dressed in a cap and gown, holding the wheelchair and grinning that big smile.

"You made it!" Sheila cried. "Congrats, Queenie!"

"And congrats to you, girl," Mary said as she began to push Sheila's chair down the long aisle, "for making a good choice."

"What, to help you out?" Sheila asked as they rolled to the handicapped section in the front row of the graduating class.

"No. For deciding to quit collecting these." Mary dropped a small plastic bag in Sheila's lap and sat down in a folding chair beside her. Sheila picked up the bag. In it were twenty-nine pain pills. "Found them under your mattress that first morning before I woke you."

After a long moment Sheila said, "I guess you knew what I really needed."

"Somebody knew." Mary smiled. "Come on. Let's go get some diplomas."

And they did.

Chapter 4

Balancing Priorities

Above all,
carefully guard your heart,
for it is the wellspring
of your life!
As you grow in wisdom
and apply your heart
to understanding,
you'll learn what is right, just, and fair
and how to make good choices.
Discretion will protect you, and
understanding will guard you.
When you delight in Me,
I'll give you the things
your heart truly desires.

BLESSINGS,
YOUR GOD OF LOVE

—from Proverbs 4:23; 2:2–11; Psalm 37:4

It has been said that the future is like a walk on a windy day. You can hide from each gust, drawing your coat ever closer around you, or you can take joy in the way the wind makes the trees sway and the leaves dance.

Carefulness or caring: Which is more important?

They are the twin oars that move us safely but passionately through life. They are the compass points that keep us on course. Living a life that is

careful and yet fully committed
to care for others is a delicate
balance. Dangers are real, and more
than one pilgrim has been blown off
course because he or she threw caution
to the wind and ignored a coming
storm.

Loving will always be risky busi-
ness. So guard your heart as precious
and holy, but offer it fully to the
friends who grace your life.

*Lord, let me be careful
but full of care. Guide me
that I may live fully
and love wisely.*

Love is a beautiful flower that blossoms on earth, with its roots embedded in eternity.

—Marvea Johnson

"You are on the dog level of Cantonese," Grandma Rose had explained one day. "You know what is spoken to you, but you cannot answer back!"

"You are on the dog level of Cantonese," Grandma Rose had explained one day. "You know what is spoken to you, but you cannot answer back!"

Small Heart, Close Heart

"Over the river and through the woods to Grandmother's house we go…" The line from the old song had gotten stuck in an endless loop in Soo Lin's head again. She smiled to herself as the Golden Gate Bridge came into view: The writers of that song had never met her Grandma Rose. As she pulled her car into the toll lane, the lyrics she had devised for that song as a child came back: "Over the Bay Bridge through Chinatown to Grandmother's house we go…"

Soo Lin's mother began to scramble for her purse to get the change for the toll. "Mom, you don't need to do that anymore." Soo Lin said, tapping the little transmitting device that automatically deducted money from their account each time they drove through one of the growing number of toll booths on the California freeways.

"I keep forgetting. Technology! What will they come up with next?" Her mother shut her purse and flipped down the visor to check her makeup. She always got a little tense when they were heading to Grandma Rose's place. Soon the hilly streets of Chinatown were all around them. They passed shops that looked as if they had been there since the Gold Rush had turned San Francisco from a dirt-poor outpost to a shining "city on the hill." Merchants with signs in Chinese offered spices and ancient herbal remedies that only the older population in this little section of the city understood or cared about. But this was Grandma Rose's corner of the world. Technology was making no inroads here. She had laughed out loud when her granddaughter had tried to talk her into a computer.

"Foolishness!" she had muttered in her native Cantonese. "Should I take my brain out and put it on a shelf? I can make my own decisions without the help of a box of wires."

"But Grandma Rose, if you had a computer, I could e-mail you," Soo Lin had argued.

"What? To tell me you don't have time to come visit? I want to see your face—not a TV screen."

Soo Lin had considered mentioning the new video phone technology, but she knew at heart that her grandmother was right. Every technological advance brought new ways to communicate without touching one another. The digital revolution was substituting bytes for hugs and e-mails for visits. But Grandma Rose was a fearless warrior in the battle for human contact. When Soo Lin had gotten so busy during her sophomore year in high school that she had not called or seen her grandmother for several weeks, Grandma Rose had sent her a letter—make that a summons—on beautiful scented stationery:

My dear Soo Lin,

Are you dead? If not, please prove this by coming to my house for Kung Po chicken this weekend.

Yours truly,
Grandma Rose

Balancing Priorities

You never had to ask Grandma Rose twice what she was thinking. "What happened to all that Asian reserve and shyness that Chinese women are supposed to have?" Soo Lin teased her one afternoon.

"Sorry. I was gone the day that was passed out," Grandma Rose had said with a wink.

Soo Lin turned onto Lake Street and parked in front of #333. Her grandmother's small yard was ablaze in flowers. It looked like a rainbow had crash-landed in her garden. Her green thumb was notorious in her neighborhood, and Grandma Rose kept her friend's tables supplied with bouquets of the most gorgeous blossoms all year long. "That's what I love about San Francisco weather," Grandma Rose often said. "You can pick a fresh flower any day of the year."

Soo Lin pulled carefully to the curb and set the parking brake on the steep hill as her mother took one last look in the mirror. Soo Lin glanced in her mirror as well. Her dark eyes and jet-black hair were about the only things that would have identified her as being partly Asian, though technically she was Eurasian. ("Like Tiger Woods? Cool," one classmate had said with admiration.) Grandma Rose, on the other hand, was 100-percent Chinese. She had met and married Soo Lin's grandfather during World War II, and after the fighting was over, he brought his new bride to his home state. Since 1946, she had lived, worked, and raised three daughters in San Francisco. Soo Lin's mother, the youngest of the three girls, looked the least Asian of the group, but Soo Lin had tapped into some of those recessive genes and was a striking mix of East and West. She locked and alarmed the car and walked arm in arm with her mother up the steps to Grandma Rose's front door.

Grandma Rose had sent her most recent "summons" letter three weeks ago. Her age and her health were not cooperating, and so attending Soo Lin's graduation ceremony down in the valley was just out of the question. The combination of the long ride and the hot sun was more than she could handle. But Grandma wanted to have her moment with the graduate before the big day. "Bring your mother and try to be here by noon." Soo Lin rang the bell and glanced at her watch: It was 11:58—Grandma Rose would be impressed.

"You're early!" a shrill voice called as she began to unlock the series of deadbolts that protected her from the ever-changing outside world.

"Hello, Momma," Soo Lin's mother said in Cantonese when the big door finally swung open. She hugged Rose's neck and stepped aside so she could greet Soo Lin.

"Hi, Grandma Rose! You look great," Soo Lin said without needing to exaggerate: Grandma Rose did look great. She was wearing a floral print dress that looked as if it could have been plucked straight from her front yard. Her jet-black hair was pulled back into a tight bun, and her eyes gleamed like little black pearls.

"I had to get dressed up for the big graduate. Don't want you to be embarrassed at Loo Fong's." Grandma had made reservations at her favorite Chinese restaurant. Reservations weren't actually needed, but she had called Pat Fong and asked her to prepare Cantonese duck for this special lunch.

"Let's get going. If they overcook the duck, we may as well eat Kentucky Fried Chicken!"

The lunch was delightful. Grandma Rose was in rare form—telling stories, partly in Cantonese and partly in English, about her childhood in China and her school years in Singapore. Soo Lin couldn't speak much of her grandmother's native tongue, but she could understand almost every word. ("You are at the dog level of Cantonese," Grandma Rose had explained one day. "You know what is spoken to you, but you cannot answer back!")

The duck was indeed delicious, and as the lunch drew to a close, Mrs. Fong brought a plate of fortune cookies to the table. Grandma Rose took the tray and offered one to her daughter, took one for herself, and extended the last one to Soo Lin. As she lifted it from the tray, it felt heavier than expected, and when she cracked it open, she knew why. A beautiful cloisonné heart had somehow been tucked inside it, along with the normal fortune strip. Soo Lin looked up at her grandmother, who was smiling a mischievous smile. "Now that's what I call a fortune," she said.

Soo Lin read the little slip of paper that had been wrapped around the heart. It was not the typical printed type, but rather it was handwritten in her grandmother's unmistakable printing. It read, "Small heart, Close heart."

Soo Lin looked with confusion at her grandmother. "I was going to write it in Chinese, but I knew you couldn't read it," Grandma Rose said with a grin.

Soo Lin spoke the words out loud: "Small heart, close heart." Then it hit her: In Chinese, word characters are combined to express other ideas. *Small heart* were the two Chinese words that together meant "be careful." *Close heart* on the other hand meant "to care for someone."

"Be careful and care?" Soo Lin asked in broken but understandable Cantonese.

"Very good." Rose patted her daughter's hand. "At least *your* daughter will teach her children some Cantonese."

"Oh Momma, you know I tried." Soo Lin's mother said.

Though none of her daughters had much of an ear for the intricacies of the spoken Chinese, Soo Lin was the best of the three.

"But what does it mean, Grandma Rose?" Soo Lin asked.

Rose took off her glasses and laid them beside her plate. "That heart was a gift from my grandmother when my family moved to Singapore. She was too frail and too set in her ways to come with us. But she wanted me to always remember China. Her brother was a craftsman—he made that heart himself. When she gave it to me, she asked me to do two things in my new home: Be careful but be full of care. *Small heart, close heart.*" Rose said these last words in Cantonese. As she said the words, she tightened her right hand into a fist while placing her left hand, fully opened, on her heart. "It means be careful of things and people that may hurt you, but never stop caring. These are the two most important things you must do…as you go on to college with all your computers and e-mails."

Soo Lin turned the beautiful heart over in her hand. On the back were the four Chinese characters for the words:

Balancing Priorities

Small heart, close heart. She looked with love at her grandmother, who was letting a rare public tear escape her eye, and she repeated the Chinese words and then the English.

" 'Be careful but full of care.' I will, Grandma Rose. I promise." Soo Lin squeezed the little heart pendant tightly in her right hand and reached out with her left to embrace her grandmother with tears of her own.

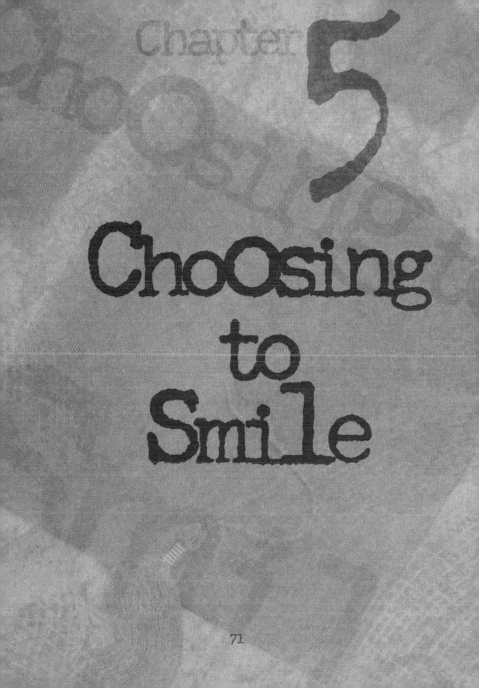

Chapter 5

Choosing to Smile

Always aim for kindness,
even when you've been wronged.
Being wronged doesn't justify
a wrong response.
The key is
letting your love abound
more and more in
knowledge and
depth of insight,
So that you may be able
to discern what is best
and may be pure and blameless

until the day of Christ Jesus.

LOVE ALWAYS,
YOUR GOD OF FORGIVENESS

—from 1 Thessalonians 5:15; Philippians 1:9–10

It has been said that truly great people are those who have learned not only to be responsible but to be "response-able." The former is the quality of faithfulness in your assigned duties. The latter is the ability to choose how you will respond to life's challenges. Disappointments and mistreatment are impossible to avoid. But the spirit with which we respond makes all the difference in how those experiences bless or bruise us.

Living the life of a doormat, accepting disrespect and scorn as normal, is not a virtue to be sought, but revenge and defensiveness can be just as damaging to our souls. Look for the path that handles libel with a laugh and responds to scorn with a smile. When we find the humor in the bleakest moments, we have also found the secret to enduring them.

God, help me smile at my enemies and disarm their hatred with humor.

There is wonderful freedom
and joy in coming to recognize
that the fun is in the becoming.
—Gloria Gaither

If he messed up now,
he might even get
kicked out
of the assembly.

A Moment to Remember

It really had been Jack's idea from the start.

Eric repeated this to himself again and again as the little lump in his shirt pocket moved once more. It was amazing that no one had noticed it. He had made it all the way to the rows of seats in the front of the field house that were reserved for the graduating class. From here he had a clear view of the whole gym. It had been decorated in red and blue crepe-paper flowers—the work of the Junior League Girls. Eric's sister would be part of that select group next year. But tonight she and his parents were sitting high up in the bleachers. His dad would have the binoculars, and his mom would be clutching her package of tissues. If his mother had known what resided in his pocket today, she would have needed more than tissues. But if the plan went well, she'd never have to know.

The whole thing had been concocted over a Grande Burrito special at Manny's Cantina three weeks before graduation. Jack Freeman, Steve Santa Ana, and Todd Perkins had all gathered for their regular Friday Mexican lunch.

"It's just not fair!" Jack mumbled as he stabbed at his burrito with a vengeance.

"What's not fair?" Eric asked. The last to arrive, he waved to Manny behind the counter as he took his seat next to Jack.

"Life!" Steve shot back as Todd nodded vigorously. "Life...and Liz Slater." The very mention of that name brought another grunt from Jack and a final vicious jab into his battered burrito. Liz Slater was the editor of the school newspaper and head of the student graduation committee. And it was she who had devised the brilliant idea of picking the student to give the graduation address by "blind essay submission." The theme was "A Moment to Remember," and any student who wanted could submit an essay for the committee to review. The names would be left off the review copies so that, as Liz said, "the best person would be chosen devoid of the politics that often taint such decisions."

The plan had not produced the results Liz had hoped for. When the votes were counted, the winning essay belonged to none other than Jack Freeman—the opinion-page editor for the school's paper and Liz Slater's least favorite person. Nearly every one of Jack's highly amusing articles had managed to offend Liz or one of her friends at some point during his two-year stint in that job. Liz had tried to get him booted off the editorial staff so many times it was a running joke at each meeting. "So what are you going to try to get me fired for this week, Lizzy?" Jack would croon.

When it was revealed that Jack had been chosen to give the graduation speech, you would have thought Pee Wee Herman had been elected "Man of the Century." Half of the student body was appalled, while the other half just shook their heads and grinned in anticipation of what would surely be the most entertaining speech in the school's history.

And Elizabeth Slater was livid. "Jack Freeman, if you embarrass me or this school…" she had ranted one day.

"Lizzy! Put your ax away, sweetie. I promise I won't embarrass you." And Eric knew Jack meant it. Jack secretly admired Liz's talents and had even asked her out once, but the socialite would never give him the time of day.

"So what's up with Liz Slater?" Eric asked as Manny brought him his regular Grande special.

"She got Jack kicked off the graduation program," Todd said.

"No way!"

"Not only that," Steve added through a mouthful of burrito. "She went behind his back to Mr. Bryan and told him Jack was going to embarrass the whole administration with some prank."

"And," Todd chimed in, "she's gonna pass it off as Jack's idea. Like he wanted her to speak in his place."

"You've got to be joking," Eric exclaimed.

"She's won this one, guys," Jack said softly. "And there's nothing I can do about it."

"Why don't you just expose her, Jack? Write an article and let her have it."

"And what would that get me? A few more enemies."

"But, Jack, we gotta do something," Steve and Todd said nearly in stereo.

"Well, I did have one idea...but I would need some help."

"All right, let's hear it," Eric said, pushing the remains of his burrito aside.

"I heard from Karen Peters that Liz has had her speech planned for some time. She's gonna bring this paper bag, and at the big moment in her speech, she's gonna reach in and pull out her baby shoes to make a sentimental point about all the steps of our lives."

"So?" asked Eric.

"I just thought we might give her a little surprise when she reaches in the bag."

Big silly grins began to spread across the conspirators' faces.

"The only problem is I don't sit near her at the assembly.

However, I managed to get a peek at the seating chart, and guess who sits right behind little Miss Speech Stealer?" Jack slowly turned to stare at Eric....

"All rise for the pledge of allegiance," Mr. Bryan said with a wave of his hands. Eric stood carefully and placed his hand over his heart. This was it. He felt the little lump shift as he touched his robe and knew this wasn't going to be as easy as Jack had made it seem that day over burritos. He shot a quick glance at Jack three rows away. Jack just nodded and said with his eyes, "You can do it, man!"

Standing directly in front of Eric, clutching her big speech in her left hand, was Liz Slater. And sitting under her chair was the infamous little brown bag. This was the moment Eric had been running through in his mind all day. If he messed up now, he might even get kicked out of the assembly. But just as his courage was wavering, Liz Slater turned and shot a smug smile at Jack Freeman, who just smiled back and winked. "Jack the Jerk," she muttered loud enough for others to hear.

OK, Liz, Eric thought, *It's time for justice.* As the pledge began, he reached up to find the end of his tassel and gave it a little tug. His cap tumbled to the ground, and as he bent down to retrieve it, he made certain no one was watching him. He shot his hand into his pocket and retrieved Clarence, his sister's pet frog, and dropped him into the bag with Liz's baby shoes. Eric stood back up just as the pledge was winding down and tried to keep from smiling too broadly as he joined the rest: "and justice for all."

The next few minutes seemed to move in slow motion. The student band did their normal, slightly-out-of-tune version of the school anthem. Mr. Bryan made a few dry comments, and then it was time. Liz Slater rose and headed for the stage, carrying her little paper bag. As she passed Jack's row, she gave him one more triumphant grin and mounted the stage.

"As most of you know, Jack Freeman was originally chosen to give this address, but he felt that what I have to say was what you needed to hear, and I thank him for that." Jack just smiled, and there was scattered applause. Jack glanced back at Eric, who gave him the prearranged thumbs-up sign.

"I stand before you today," Liz went on, "with a treasure

beside me." She gestured to the paper bag, and as she did, it moved ever so slightly. Eric thought he would choke, but Liz didn't seem to notice. "What I am about to show you represents the steps that you and I have made and will make as we move toward our future. Do any of you remember these…"

Then she did it: Liz Slater reached into her little brown bag and pulled out a pair of baby shoes…with a fully grown toad sitting in one of them. Clarence, the toad, let out a perfectly timed croak and leaped onto the podium. Liz stood frozen, staring at the green creature. And then she made her biggest mistake of the evening: She screamed. Clarence, who doesn't take well to loud noises, leaped from the podium and onto Liz's graduation gown, disappearing under her collar. Liz panicked, began flailing at the zipper of her gown, backed into the band director's music stand, and fell into the first-chair flute player's lap. It was at that moment that Clarence, who must have been just as frightened as Liz, managed to hop out of her gown and land squarely on the second-chair flutist's lap. At this, the whole flute section broke into pandemonium, and in the crash of folding chairs and falling music stands, Liz Slater managed to crawl right into the bass drum stand, which collapsed on her unceremoniously.

Mr. Bryan was still trying to determine what had happened when Jack made it to the podium. His timing was nothing short of perfect.

"Thanks, Liz," Jack said loudly into the microphone, "for helping with that little stunt. Relax, folks, we've had this planned for some time. I think we fooled them all, Liz!"

Mr. Byran stared at Jack and then turned to look at Liz, who was still trying to extricate herself from the bass drum stand with the tuba player's help. The senior class began to laugh, and when Steve and Todd started applauding, it swept across the whole audience.

One of the trumpet players had managed to catch Clarence, and he walked up and handed the toad over to Jack. Liz, who was finally back on her feet and trying to figure out what had happened, saw everyone applauding and did the only think she could think to do: She bowed.

"Wasn't she convincing, folks? Come here, Liz." Jack called. And the applause grew louder. As she reached the podium, Jack put his arm around her and whispered, "Stick with me, and you'll get out of this OK." Then he turned to the audience and said seriously, "This little lady and I just wanted you all to know that life is not just a series of baby steps, for many occasions require us to take great leaps! Right, Liz?" Liz nodded vigorously, praying it was the right choice. "And beginning today, you and I are taking one of the biggest leaps. We are leaping into the future…"

And with that Jack Freeman began the speech of a lifetime. The student body stopped him five times with thunderous applause. When he finished, he shook Liz's hand, and they both took one more bow before marching back toward their seats to a standing ovation. As he was helping her down the steps, Liz leaned close to Jack and whispered, "Why did you do that? You could have made a fool of me."

Jack grinned his trademark grin and said, "Oh no, I was just looking for a way for both of us to leave here with a moment to remember." And with that, he hugged her and headed for his seat, pondering whether Liz Slater might want a Coke after the graduation assembly.

Chapter 6

Letting Go

I know you better
than anyone else.
I'm familiar with all of your ways.
You can't begin
to Comprehend
My precious thoughts of you.
Even before you were conceived,
I ordained all of your days
with purpose.
I'll instruct you
and teach you
in the way that you should go,
Counseling you and
watching over you.
When you're discouraged or afraid,
remember I'm with you
twenty-four hours a day,
wherever you go!

LOVE,
YOUR GOD AND BEST FRIEND

—from Psalms 139:1–18; 32:8; Joshua 1:9

Friendships are the spice that makes life worth living. They give us hope and confidence to face whatever tomorrow may bring. But if we cling too tightly to those we care for, we underestimate the power of the bond. Time forges great friendships that will not wither in a season. There is something wonderful to be found in friendships that have stood the test of distance and age. Good friends have the amazing ability to go through long times apart and then pick up right where they left off.

Trust your friendships to be enduring. Value the bonds that have been built over time. Keep investing in those relationships: call, write, visit. Above all else, believe in the commitment of caring, and trust the integrity of love. It will prove hardier than tough times and mightier than miles.

Thank you, Lord, for the friends who've blessed my life and shaped my soul.

Simple pleasures of growing up together are preserved in the keepsake albums of our hearts.

—Jane Debord

Their friendship was
too **rich**,
too deep
for physical attraction
to louse it up.

friendship

Their **friendship** wa
too **rich**,
too deep
for physical attraction
to louse it up.

Best Friends

"Got one!" Teri shouted and held up the tiny shell for Rick to see. He squinted in the sunshine and was about to declare it empty when he caught a glimpse of the little legs of a hermit crab retreating into the curve of the shell. She had beaten him...just like always.

"OK, but I bet I can get five before you do!"

"You're on, loser!" Teri called back and bent over the tide pools again.

This part of the beach had always been their sanctuary. Rick tried to remember the first time he had seen her here. They were both in fourth grade, and Pacific Elementary's field trip to the ocean had been the highlight of the year. Fifty squealing eight-year-olds leaping from tide pool to tide pool, discovering new treasures at every turn. He saw her leaning over a shallow cut in one rock that held several large sea anemones. Her long, red hair nearly touched the water as she peered at the strange-looking creatures.

"If you poke your finger in them, they disappear," Rick said from behind her.

"Don't be silly," she replied without looking up. "Just 'cause I moved here from Kansas doesn't mean I don't know about sea stuff."

"No, I'm not kidding. Stick your finger in the middle, and you'll see."

Teri looked at him with narrow-eyed skepticism. "You do it first."

"OK," Rick said and squatted down next to her. "But if it sucks me in, tell the teacher so my mom and dad will know what happened to me." Teri rolled her eyes but watched closely as Rick reached into the salt water and gently poked one of the smaller creatures right in the center of its body. As soon as his finger touched its feelers, the animal balled up into a tiny knot, nearly disappearing in the sand.

"It's pulling me in," Rick screamed in mock horror, holding his finger against the animal. "Help me please!" Teri panicked, grabbed Rick by the arm, and pulled with all her weight. They both tumbled onto the sand and Rick laughed out loud. Seeing that she had been duped, she splashed a handful of water in Rick's direction.

"You're a creep!"

"I'm sorry. You just looked so scared!" He wiped the water off his face and stuck out his hand in gesture of peace, "I'm Ricky Satterfield."

"I'm Teri Graves." They shook hands and became instant friends.

Through the years, they had seen each other through losing tonsils and losing grandparents. Rick had been there for Teri when her parents divorced, and Teri had been Rick's support when his brother had nearly died as a result of a terrible motorcycle accident during his first year of college.

Some friends predicted they would end up dating, but it

just never came to pass. Rick always believed it was because their friendship was too rich, too deep for physical attraction to louse it up. So instead, they became closer than brother and sister. No one was surprised when Teri, as homecoming queen, asked Rick to be her escort. Theirs had been a story-book friendship...till now.

"Done!" Teri shouted just as Rick nabbed his final crabby victim. "I've got five too. I just didn't yell fast enough." He held out his hand as proof, and as he did, one of the crabs scurried over his palm and fell back into the surf.

"I believe you have four," Teri said with mock disap-proval.

They dropped all the crabs into an empty soda cup Rick had found and sat like little children watching the crabs climb over one another trying to find a way out of their Styrofoam prison.

"Remember when we decided to take some home and start a crab farm?"

Teri grimaced, "Ohhhh, I had managed to wipe that memory from my mind."

"You were the one who said we could keep them alive in a cup. The next morning I told my mom they were just sleeping. It wasn't until they started to smell that she convinced me they were dead."

"We had a burial at sea. That I do remember." They sat in a comfortable silence for several minutes, watching the surf and thinking about the past.

"Those were good times. Sometimes I wish I could just go back and stay there," Rick finally said.

"Me too."

"But times change, huh?"

"Yeah." Teri wanted to say more but didn't know how. When she had let Rick know of her decision to attend Davidson University in North Carolina instead of Berkley with him, he hadn't handled it well.

"If you wanted to avoid me, you didn't have to pick a college on the other side of the country!" he had said with more than a little sarcasm in his voice. She had started several times to defend her choice, but somehow knew it would just add insult to injury. They were too close for logical rationales or self-defensive explanations. They had always trusted each other's love, and this time could be no different.

"I've been thinking a lot about this fall," Rick said, poking down one of the crabs who had nearly reached the rim of the cup. "It's hard to imagine not seeing you every week."

"You're telling me," Teri said with a sigh. "Yesterday, my mother gave me the picture of us the summer we did the junior life-saving camp."

"That one with those goofy sunglasses?"

"That's it. She had it framed for me to take to Davidson and left it on my dresser. I cried like a baby when I saw it."

"You'll be fine," Rick said, placing his hand on her knee.

"And so will you," Teri said softly. Then she added, "And so will we." She slipped her hand around his, and they sat in silence again.

"Promise me you won't make any stupid decisions without calling me first," Rick said.

"Me? You're the one I'm worried about! What about Sylvia Perkins?"

"Teri, you don't want to go there! Do I need to mention Jeff Timmons? Or Brad Henegar? Or Barry Ross?"

"OK, OK. I promise to call you before making any stupid decisions."

"And I promise to tell you not to be stupid."

"And do you promise not to quit caring just 'cause I'm three thousand miles away?"

Rick looked at Teri and then at the cup full of crabs. "There are some things you can't hold too tightly. If you try, they just die." He slowly poured the captive crabs back out into the closest tide pool where they disappeared as soon as they hit the water. "Your only choice is to let go and trust that they will be there the next time you come looking."

Teri leaned over and hugged him tightly, and he held her even tighter. As they did, they could almost feel a chapter of their lives closing as another began. They walked the beach one last time: best friends…for always.

Chapter 7

Healing Hurts

I'm working in you to will
and act according to
My good and perfect will.
Trust in Me With all your heart.
Don't rely on your own
limited understanding.

Remember, I have the advantage
of seeing the entire picture!
When you acknowledge Me
in all you say and do,
I'll faithfully
direct your steps.

Guiding You,
Your God of Wisdom

—from Philippians 2:13; Proverbs 3:5–6

Love is a double-edged sword. It brings the greatest joys and the greatest pains people can know. It wants to hold and nurture, to rescue and protect. This is its nature.

But moments of growth and steps toward maturity will often be taken against the pull of those we love. Don't let this fool you: Love is not the enemy. Give thanks for those who care for you and seek to guard your way. See them not as obstacles, but as opportunities to grow and love in a different way.

Be gentle as apron strings are cut and wings are tested. Be firm when the call of God on your heart leads you to places that love may find threatening or even frightening. And quietly remind your heart that someday you, too, will cling with loving arms to someone or something that deserves to fly.

Let me love those who love me with the respect I seek and the tenderness they deserve.

There is a path before you
that you alone can walk.
There is a purpose that you
alone can fulfill.
　　　—Karla Dornacher

scholarship

When the college's
dean of admissions
called with a
full scholarship,
the dream turned into
a nightmare.

When the college's
dean of admissions
called with a
full scholarship,
the dream turned into
a nightmare.

Picture Perfect

Cathy and her mother circled the town square one more time. At three o'clock on a Friday afternoon, parking spots were at a premium in the tiny downtown. The ride from the farm had been silent, but it was better than the alternative. Any conversation she had tried to have with her mom over the last six months had ended the same way: Cathy in tears and her mother in silence.

Thankfully, the taillights on an old blue Chevy (an Impala, Cathy thought) signaled that whoever owned it was about to vacate his precious space. Cathy whipped around the square to get in position to grab the spot.

"We do have a speed limit in this town," her mother said curtly. Cathy slowed down without a word. "Not like the big city where you can drive as you like, do as you please, and nobody cares."

Cathy eased the truck into the spot and turned off the engine. "You want to come in with me?"

"You go ahead. My opinion doesn't seem to count for much these days."

"Mom, please. Can't we have a truce?"

Cathy's mom was silent again. Cathy heaved a sigh and got out of the truck alone. She wished she were already at college in California and that the little town square of Highfield was far away.

No more driving two hours just to get to a mall.

No more choosing from the same two places to eat every Friday night.

No more getting recognized as "Jack and Sarah Williams's little girl" everywhere she went.

But her mother had amassed a different list. From the time Cathy had told her of the scholarship offer from

Pepperdine, she had started working on it. By now it ran for several pages, but the top three were always the same.

No more safety net for friends and family to catch her if she fell.

No more dinners with the family every Sunday after church.

And, most important, no more mother to watch and pray over her every move.

"There is no way in the world that I am going to let my last child go halfway around the world to some heathen city for college. If Cleburn Community was good enough for your brother Jimmy…" Her brother had dutifully attended the closest school to the family and the farm and was well on his way to becoming a true "Highfield-er." Cathy had coined the term for the folks in town who saw no reason to stray from its confining borders more than necessary. And Jimmy was happy with that. Working at the Piggly Wiggly and helping Dad at harvest time was his idea of a great life. "I might even be a manager in a few years," he had informed her at dinner one night.

For a while, Cathy thought she was the problem. There must be something wrong with her crazy notions of living in a big city far from the comforts of Highfield and home. But whenever Mr. Acuff put out the new travel magazines at his drugstore, she was the first to snatch one up. New York. Los Angeles. London. Paris. She could see herself living in any one of them. Any place with a subway, a symphony, and lots of people.

Pepperdine had been a bolt from the blue. A recruiter had sent her a brochure because of her stellar scores on the SAT. (Even her normally stoic father had raised an eyebrow. "Top 1 percent in the country. Ain't that something?") Cathy had quietly filled out the response card and returned it. Malibu, California, seemed like an impossible dream to her, but what's wrong with a little dreaming now and then? When the college's dean of admissions called with a full scholarship, the dream turned into a nightmare.

"Absolutely not!" her mother had pronounced with uncommonly twisted logic: "If they are willing to let kids go for free, then it can't be much of a college. Must be pretty hard up for students." It had steadily gotten worse from there.

Cathy dropped a quarter into the parking meter, gave one more pleading look to her mother sitting stonefaced in the cab, and went alone into Bently's Photography. Mr. Bently looked up as the bell that his father's father had hung above the door rang and announced her entrance. "Well, Cathy Williams. Been waiting to show you these," Frank Bently said excitedly. "Better not let the boys around here see these, or you'll never make it out to California!"

"Are you sure you're talking about my pictures, Mr. Bently?" Cathy took a seat at the counter where countless students had sat to review their senior portraits. Mr. Bently placed a large white folder in front of her with great care.

"You look for yourself. Just don't get your fingerprints on them."

Mr. Bently had not been exaggerating: Cathy's pictures were breathtaking. Her auburn hair cascaded around her face, forming a perfect frame. And the photographer had managed to capture the expression of dreamy optimism that was the essence of her personality.

"I hope those folks in Malibu are ready for you."

"Well, Malibu seems a long ways off today."

Mr. Bently glanced out at the parked truck and nodded. "Your mom still not letting go?"

"Does everybody in this town know everything about my life?"

"This is Highfield, Cathy. People care. Just remember, your mom wanted to do the same thing herself."

Cathy stopped looking at the pictures and turned to Mr. Bently. "What did you say?"

A mischievous smile crossed Frank Bently's face. "Wait a minute." He disappeared into the back of his shop and came out with a dusty envelope.

"Came across these when I was cleaning out some files this spring. Was gonna give them to your dad to surprise your mom, but I never got around to it."

Cathy opened the folder and let out a low sigh. She had

the strange sensation that she was looking at herself, but it was her mother's face smiling back at her as she had never known her: as a senior in high school. A bright, perky smile was on her lips, and she had her head cocked at an angle that almost said, "You'll never guess what all I'm going to do."

"Your mom was something. Broke every heart in town when she announced she was going to Philadelphia."

"My mother was going to Philadelphia?"

"Oh yeah. Big art school up there. Thought she might be the next Rembrandt, I guess. They were going to give her a free ride. Too bad. Her momma died just two months before she was supposed to leave."

"She never told me any of that," Cathy said in a stupor.

"Oh my goodness. I've done it now." He snatched back the pictures as though he could somehow take back what had been revealed.

"Please. May I have them?"

Mr. Bently looked out at the truck again. "I suppose they might come in handy. Eh?"

Cathy smiled and nodded, and Mr. Bently slid the yellowing folder back to her. "Good luck, Cathy. Your mom loves you a lot."

"I know that," she said looking at the folder of pictures and deciding what to do. "And the pictures look great. Thanks, Mr. Bently. The one you had on top will be perfect."

Cathy signed a form and selected the number of copies she wanted then made her way back out to the truck.

"Pictures turn out all right?" her mother asked as she shut the door.

"They were OK, but not as good as these." Cathy laid the photographs in her mother's lap.

"Oh my word," her mother said as she opened the folder and began thumbing through the pictures. "What was that crazy Frank Bently doing showing you these?"

"They're beautiful, Mom. You were a lovely girl—with a bright future."

Cathy's mom looked up from the pictures and then back toward the photography shop.

"Philadelphia is a long way from here," Cathy said softly. "Nearly as far as California."

Sarah Williams lowered her head.

"I guess I should have been able to figure out between the date of Granny Matthews's death and your graduation, but the art scholarship—why didn't you tell me?"

"Fools thought I could draw. They would have learned different."

"Maybe not. But you'll never know, will you?"

"Are you judging my choices?"

"No, Mom. Not for a minute. God gave each of us the right to make our own choices. And those who love us should respect that."

Words formed on Cathy's mom's lips, but they never made it out. As the tears came, she leaned toward her daughter and held her tightly. Cathy's tears mingled with her mother's, and they both sat hugging and crying in the cab of the truck parked in the middle of Highfield town square. When words did come, Cathy's mom began: "I just want you to be all right. I love you so much."

"I know, Mom. I love you too. And I'll be all right." After another hug, Cathy picked up one of the pictures. "Can I have one of these?"

"Sure. But if you put it up in that dorm room in Malibu, you'll have to tell the boys I'm already taken."

Cathy looked at her mom with a mixture of surprise and relief. "Oh, Momma!" And they hugged again.

"All right, let's get going. I want to show these to your father. He's probably forgotten what a good choice he made!"

They laughed together for the first time in months as Cathy backed out the truck and headed for home.